D1527847

SINGAPORE TRAVEL GUIDE

**HUNGRY
PASSPORT**

How to use this guide?

SECTIONS ARE DIVIDED BY COLORS

SECTION I

Things to know before you go

Packed with practical info from how to get from the airport to Singapore, how to get around the city, the best time to visit, the best apps to use, which tours to take, etc.

SECTION II & III

Top 10 attractions & 10 additional ones

The absolute must-see 10 attractions, especially if you are visiting for the first time. If you have more time, find additional impressive landmarks and experiences.

SECTION IV

Itineraries, Day trips Things to do when...

If you don't have the time to plan your own itinerary, you'll find things to do if it's raining, if it's too hot, in the evening, and more.

THIS GUIDE IS INTERACTIVE

Scan the QR code

- **Maps**
- **Tickets**
- **Apps**
- **Info**

TABLE OF CONTENTS

Main MAP

Includes top 10, additional 10 attractions & more

- **A** Gardens by the Bay
- **B** Singapore Flyer
- **C** Marina Bay
- **D** Chinatown
- **E** Fort Canning Park
- **F** Bugis Street
- **G** Kampong Glam
- **H** Little India
- **I** Sentosa
- **J** Henderson Waves
- **K** Botanic Gardens
- **L** TreeTop Walk

Things to Know Before You Go to Singapore

This section includes:

GENERAL INFO

Quick Facts & Info

Population: 5.45 million (2021)

Land area: 728 km²

Languages: English (de facto), Malay (de jure), Chinese, Tamil, etc.

Best time to visit: A year-round destination, but best between February and April (driest season)

For how long: 3 days

Covid-19 updates

Official tourist info

Visa Info

Singapore events

Drinking Water

It is perfectly safe to drink tap water in Singapore. There's not a lot of drinking water fountains available throughout the city.

Toilets

There are many public toilets in Singapore and most of them are free. Some cost a fee to use it (10 cents), so have enough coins ready. You can still use a toilet at a bar, restaurant, etc.

Safety & Strict Rules

Crime info

Singapore is an extremely safe place for tourists but beware of pickpockets. The country is very strict with their laws for littering, chewing gum, jaywalking, smoking in public, drugs and similar.

Emergency services number: 999 or **995**

◄ **Singapore Crime rate map** (areas to avoid)

Power Plugs

Type G

Power plug used in Singapore is **Type G** - they uses British sockets.

Travel Adapters

If you are coming from outside Singapore, UK & some other countries, you will need a travel adapter to charge your phone & other devices.

Wheelchair access

Accessibility

With various government projects for accessibility, Singapore is a wheelchair friendly destination. Metro stations are equipped with priority lifts & wheelchair-accessible toilets.

◄ **Wheelchair accessible guide**

MONEY

Currency

$ - Singapore Dollar (S$) is the official currency of Singapore.

S$1 is worth approximately*:

$ 0.76 USD
€ 0.70 EUR
$ 0.01 CAD
$ 1.08 AUD
£ 0.62 GBP
¥ 98 JPY
₹ 62 INR
$ 14 MXN

Current rates

*Data for Jan 2023

Credit Cards

Most hotels, stores, and restaurants in the country accept major credit cards like Visa or MasterCard. It is always wise to have some cash with you especially if you plan visit local hawker centers, market and similar.

ATMs

ATMs can be found all over the city-state. For better exchange rates and smaller fees, always choose to be billed in Singapore Dollars and only use ATMs owned by banks.

WEATHER & CLIMATE

Singapore has **tropical climate** with hot and humid weather throughout the year. There is little difference in temperature between the months.

Northeast Monsoon

86 °F
30 °C
Avg. high

Northeast Monsoon season is from December to March.

Heavy rainfall usually occurs from November to January.

73 °F - 88 °F
23 °C - 31 °C
Avg. temperature

Southwest Monsoon

88 °F
31 °C
Avg. high

Southwest Monsoon occurs from June to September.

Rainfall in Singapore is often accompanied by thunder.

75 °F - 88 °F
24 °C - 31 °C
Avg. temperature

The months in between are called the **Inter-Monsoon** period. The hottest months are June and July, with December and January being the coldest.

TRANSPORTATION

From and to Singapore Changi Airport (SIN)

Singapore Changi Airport (SIN) is approximately 20 km from Marina Bay (Singapore's Downtown). You can use any of the following means of transportation:

Public Transportation ▾

Train

To the city center:

(1) from Changi Airport MRT Station (CG2) to Tanah Merah MRT Station (EW4), then transfer to the East West Line towards Tuas Link MRT Station (EW33).

(2) Changi Airport MRT Station to Expo MRT Station (CG1/DT35), then transfer to the Downtown Line towards Bukit Panjang MRT Station (BP6/DT1).

Public Bus

Terminals 1, 2 and 3 (at basement bus bays): buses 24, 27, 34, 36, 53, 110 858

Terminal 4 (bus stop next to Car Park 4B): buses 24, 34, 36 and 110. At the bus stop near the SATS Inflight Catering Centre 1, you can take buses 27, 53 and 858.

IMPORTANT: Walk or take Skytrain to move between T1, T2 & T3. Shuttle Bus takes you to T4. Jewel is located between T2 & T3, and directly connected to T1.

Shuttle

Taxi

Available for hire at the Arrival areas of T 1 & T3.

Car Rentals

We do not recommend this option.

Shuttle

Changi Airport Website

Getting AROUND THE CITY

Most of the sights in Singapore are close-by, so it is easy to get around on foot. But if you don't feel like walking, you can use the following modes of transport:

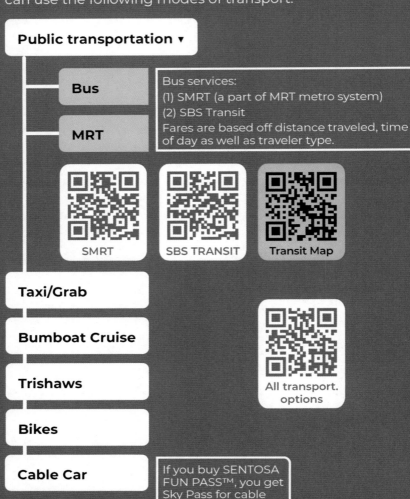

Public transportation ▼

Bus

MRT

Bus services:
(1) SMRT (a part of MRT metro system)
(2) SBS Transit
Fares are based off distance traveled, time of day as well as traveler type.

SMRT

SBS TRANSIT

Transit Map

Taxi/Grab

Bumboat Cruise

Trishaws

Bikes

Cable Car

All transport. options

If you buy SENTOSA FUN PASS™, you get Sky Pass for cable car rides

Getting AROUND THE CITY

Travel Smart Cards

If you will use a public transportation, the most convenient is to get an **EZ-Link Pass: Contactless Smart Card** It is valid for MRT trains, local buses, riverboats, Sentosa Express monorail, and even taxis. You can buy the card at any customer service counter or at any 7-Eleven for about $10. You can reload the card for a min. of $10 at any station ticket machine

You can purchase **Singapore Tourist Pass**

They have introduced **contactless payments** on trains and buses (SimplyGo) - Download app (scan the QR code below).

EZ-Link
Pass

Singapore
Tourist Pass

SimplyGo
App

ACCOMMODATION

Average hotel price/night for 2 people

From S$150
From US$**108** / €**106**

TIP 1: The price varies and depends on the location, type of facility & level of luxury (hotel/hostel/capsule), cancellation options, etc. Also, pay attention to extra charges like tourist tax, breakfast, etc.

TIP 2: You can find better deals if you take the time to research multiple online booking platforms, like Airbnb or Booking. Also, be flexible with the dates when booking. Try to book accommodation with cancellation options.

Some of the best areas to stay:

Civic District with many of the best sights, bars, and restaurants and **Clarke Quay** is great for nightlife
Marina Bay for upscale area of skyscrapers, posh hotels & luxury malls
Sentosa Island for families

If you want to save some money:

Stay at the budget hotels near Little India, Chinatown, Geylang

FOOD & DRINKS

We suggest using **Yelp** or **TripAdvisor** to find nearby places with good reviews. Try to avoid sitting down in the restaurants next to major attractions. Try delicious food at one of many hawker centers.

AVERAGE PRICES - bars, restaurants

DRINKS

Kopi Coffee*	S$ 1.2
Water	S$ 2
Juice**	S$ 2+
Beer	S$ 10
Wine	S$ 12
Cocktail	S$ 15-20

FOOD

Avg. meal	S$ 10+
Laksa	S$ 3
Satay per stick	S$ 0.5
Pandan Chiffon Cake	S$ 1.7

*Coffee at Starbucks: S$6 | **Sugarcane Juice: S$1.8, Bubble Tea: S$3, Soda: S$3*

S$ 1 = 0.76 USD or 0.70 EUR | S$ 10 = 7.60 USD or 7 EUR

Unique bars & eateries, best hawker centers, etc.

- beGIN
- Lantern
- Le Petit Chef
- The Elephant Room
- Maison Ikkoku
- Tekka Centre, etc.

See map for more ▸

View Map

GOOD TO KNOW

Tipping

Tipping is generally discouraged in Singapore. Most restaurants will have a 10% service charge already included.

Lines & Crowds

Singapore is a popular destination, so be prepared to wait in line, especially in the holiday season and around big tourist attractions. The same goes for restaurants and other public places.

You can buy a city pass where you can save on attractions and get skip the line privileges.

SIM

WIFI

Internet

You can get **free WiFi** at most hotels, metro stations, and hostels with Singapore's Wireless@SG free public WiFi. There are some outdoor and indoor hotspots in the city, including restaurants, fast food places, cafés, bars, and hotels.

You can purchase a **prepaid SIM card** or rent a **pocket WiFi** or mobile hotspot.

Singapore Specifics

Discipline is highly regarded in Singapore, so make sure not to break any of the following laws:

- **Chewing gum** is illegal in the Singapore.
- **Jaywalking** is forbidden, so make sure to find the appropriate pedestrian lane.
- Singapore is known for being clean, so they're strict against **littering and smoking** in indoor public areas and some select outdoor facilities.
- There's no eating and drinking **inside the MRT** station and inside the trains.
- Don't feed **pigeons**.
- You're required to **flush** in public toilets.

OTHER IMPORTANT INFORMATION:

- Singapore uses the **metric system**.
- People often walk and stand on the **left side** of the lane in foot traffic.
- Don't sit on the **reserved seat** on public transportation as it's seen as rude to take the place of someone who needs it like the elderly.

Visa

For tourists, a passport valid for at least six months and a return ticket is required to enter the city-state. When it comes to Visas, **most nationalities can enter for a maximum of 30 days**, such as residents of Canada, United States, European Union, Australia, New Zealand, Norway, South Korea, Switzerland, and the United Kingdom can enter visa-free for a maximum of 90 days.

Visa Link

City Passes, Tours, Views

City Passes

A great option to save money if you are planning to visit several attractions and want to skip the line at some locations.

Singapore Tourist Pass

Sentosa FUN Pass

Singapore City Pass

HIPPO SIN Pass

Go SIN Pass

Best Views of Singapore

- Singapore Flyer
- Helix Bridge
- Sands SkyPark Observation Deck
- Marina Bay Waterfront Promenade
- Gardens by The Bay
- 1-Altitude bar with a rooftop area
- Henderson Waves

See map for more ▸

View Map

City Tours, Cooking & Other Classes

A great way to discover Singapore is by a tour organized by professional guides who know a great deal about the city's culture. Some providers even offer free or pay-what-you-wish walking tours.

Tours are a perfect way to discover the city for those who would like to get a sense of the city and those with limited time in Singapore.

Book your favorite tour

Trishaw Tour: Chinatown, Little India and more

Hawker Center Food Tour in Chinatown

Creepy & Haunted Tour with Cemetery Visit

Withlocals: Highlights & Hidden Gems

Battlebox and Fort Canning Hill Tour

Walking and Food Tour in Singapore

Cultural Cooking Class

Chinatown and Little India Photo Walk

Mangrove Kayaking Adventure

BEST APPS

Restaurants, reviews and food delivery

- TripAdvisor
- Yelp
- Chope
- Grab

Do things with locals

- **Eatwith** Eat with locals
- **Withlocals** Tours, etc.
- **Airbnb** Tours, etc.
- **Meetup** Group meetings

Other apps

- **Duolingo** Learn languages
- **Visit SG** Travel guide
- **Google Translate**
- **XE Currency** Converter

Explore the city

- **Google/Apple Maps**
- **Explore SG** MRT map
- **CityMapper** Transit
- **SG Buses** Bus Guide
- **Grab** Ride, Delivery
- **TransitLink**
- **Viator** Book a tour
- **RYDE** Taxi, Carpool

Download Apps

About Singapore

Singapore is a city-state located on the Malay Peninsula. It has 5.6 million inhabitants, one main island, and 58 smaller islands. The tropical climate makes it a popular year-round destination.

Renowned for its economic prosperity and multi-cultural character, Singapore is one of Asia's major hubs. Known as one of the world's cleanest cities, Singapore is also home to the world's best airport and numerous architectural marvels and attractions.

A BRIEF HISTORY

First mentioned in the 3rd century AD as Pu Luo Chung, larger settlement of the area began in the 14th century. Sang Nila Utama, a Sumatran prince, founded the Kingdom of Singapura in 1299. The legend says that he decided to settle there after a lion-like animal briefly appeared in front of him while hunting. Considering the sighting a good sign, he named the kingdom Singapura, meaning "Lion City" in Sanskrit.

In the centuries that followed, people of Chinese, Malay, Indian, and other backgrounds started to settle there. From traders, fishermen to warriors – Singapore became a vital sea trade hub.

By the 19th century, Singapore became a British colony. Sir Thomas Stamford Raffles modernized the city, and the story of Singapore as the major trading nation and an important Asian hub began.

During WWII, Singapore was overtaken by the Japanese in 1941 and was reestablished as a British Colony in 1946. In 1964, following a failed attempt to become a part of Malaysia, Singapore became an independent country, enabling business development, and banking, placing Singapore in one of the world's economic success stories.

21

Top 20
MAPS

Top 10 Things to Do in Singapore

This section includes:

1

Guided tour

Marina Bay (Waterfront Promenade)

. . .

Waterfront for long walks and outdoor activities

Map

Marina Bay Waterfront Promenade is a great place for outdoor activities and public events. Stroll along the promenade, popular with locals and tourists, and enjoy the view of the bay and the city.

Some of the famous attractions include:

- **Merlion Park:** visit Merlion, a mythical creature of Singapore with the body of a fish and the head of a lion.
- **Marina Bay Sands:** One of the world's most famous hotels, with an observation deck, casino, malls, light and water show.
- **Art Science Museum:** A fusion of art, science, culture, and technology, first of its kind in the world.
- **Helix Bridge:** A pedestrian bridge with a view of the Singapore skyline, with four viewing platforms
- **Other attractions in Marina Bay:** Apple Marina, Esplanade Concert Hall, Bay East garden, The Float @ Marina Bay, Marina East Park, Marina Barrage, etc.

---

i **Don't miss:** Raffles Landing closeby, where the founder of Singapore Stamford Raffles landed in 1819.

2a

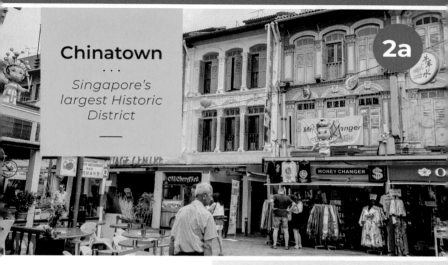

Chinatown

. . .

Singapore's largest Historic District

—

2a

Map

Rich with history and culture, this **unique ethnic quarter** creates its charm with a heritage center, temples, and traditional Chinese places.

Some original family-run restaurants and teahouses still stand there today. You can visit one of its wet markets and try authentic Chinese food.

Famous attractions ▶

- **Buddha Tooth Relic Temple:** Explore this five-story temple full of art, history, and culture of Buddhism, including a theater and teahouse.
- **Sri Mariamman Temple:** Singapore's oldest Hindu temple
- **Thian Hock Keng Temple:** the oldest Chinese temple in Singapore with traditional architecture
- **Pagoda St. & Chinatown Heritage Centre:** with its six galleries, it will take you back to the past with the stories of Singapore's earliest Chinese residents.
- **Mosque St.:** it features Masjid Jamae mosque

i **Don't miss:** Maxwell Food Centre hawker center

2b

Kampong Glam and Little India

. . .

Two unique neighborhoods

___

KAMPONG GLAM

This neighborhood is best known for housing the **Sultan Mosque** and features the Malay heritage of Singapore. You can also do some exploring in the area with boutiques and cafes in **Haji Lane** or grab some Malay and Indonesian fabrics and handmade perfumes in **Arab Street.**

LITTLE INDIA

Showcasing the country's Indian culture. Don't miss:

- **House of Tan Teng Niah:** a colorful villa from 1900s.
- **Indian Heritage Centre:** depicting Indian culture
- **Tekka Market:** home to the biggest wet market
- **Buffalo Road** with Tekka Food Centre

2b

3a

Things to Do

Sentosa
. . .
Tropical paradise with many activities

3a

Map

easily spend a day or two in this tropical getaway.

Don't miss famous beaches, such as **Siloso, Palawan, or Tanjong Beach**, and try different water and other sports.

You can reach Sentosa Island by cable car, sky-train, and a car. For the ultimate experience, choose cable cars that take you to multiple locations on the island.

Beautiful and Instagram-worthy **beaches are man-made**.

Singapore got the sand from its neighboring countries like Indonesia, Malaysia, and Cambodia and created these delightful tropical escapades.

With all-year-round sunshine and the budget-friendly beaches, you can

i **Did you know?** "Siloso" comes from the Malayan word "rock."

3b

Sentosa
· · ·
Tropical paradise with many activities
___

Fort Siloso is a remnant of a 1950s fort used in defense during World War II. Visit a military museum with artifacts from the war, such as coastal guns, the Surrender Chamber with displays of the British and Japanese Surrender, and some preserved military structures.

You can take the 11-stories high scenic route **Sky Walk**, which can be experienced with a guided tour where you can learn more about its historical significance to the country.

Magical Shores, multi-sensory experience with a light and sound spectacle: Nocturnal Awakening, Islet Whispers, Force of Nature & New Peaks.

There attractions:

- Adventure (sports): Bungy Jump, Giant Swing, Skybridge
- Other sports: iFly indoor skydiving
- SkyHelix Sentosa
- Wings of Time Lightshow
- S.E.A. Aquarium
- Universal Studios
- Adventure Cove Waterpark
- Butterfly Park
- Dolphin Island
- Golf courses & more

4a

Fort Canning
Park

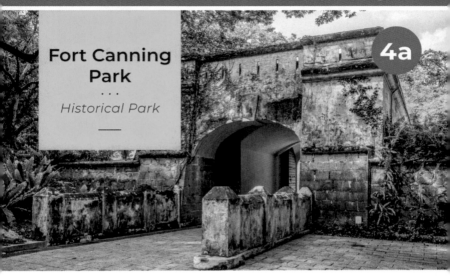

Fort Canning Park

· · ·

Historical Park

——

4a

ENTRANCE FEE

Free

OPENING HOURS

7am-7pm
Daily

Location

Fort Canning Park is the **former home of the Malay kings** and the Far East Command Centre and British Army.

Several notable historical events unfolded on this hill. Upon entering, you can't miss the **Fort Gate**, a part of a fortress from the 19th century, often used as a site for social events. Don't miss the Fort Canning Lighthouse.

The Battlebox, the site of the British's surrender of Singapore to the Japanese in World War II, has now been turned into a museum.

The Malays call this hill "Bukit Larangan" or **Forbidden Hill** because it's said to be haunted by Singapore's ancient kings. They're believed to be buried here.

i **Tip:** take a photo on the spiral staircase

4b

Fort Canning Park

. . .

Historical Park

——

Fort Caning park houses **nine gardens**. Some of the most interesting ones are:

Sang Nila Utama Garden

A garden that integrates traditional Malay or Javanese culture in its structure, design, and plants.

Raffles Garden

Named after the founder of modern Singapore, this garden features plants from the Southeast Asia region.

Artisan's Garden

A garden dating back to the 14th century. It is the site of one of the last archeological digs in the country.

4b

5a

Shopping
Websites

Shopping
. . .
*Singapore,
a shopping
paradise*

5a

___

CLARKE QUAY

Where the nightlife of Singapore comes to life with numerous restaurants, bars, and clubs. By day, Clarke Quay is a shopping spot offering various shops and malls.

BUGIS STREET MARKET

It offers a wide variety of options with bazaars in every corner selling souvenir items, home supplies, clothing and food (3 floors with over 600 shops). Don't skip the nearby **Bugis+** and **Bugis Junction.**

ORCHARD ROAD

Center of shopping and retail offers a myriad of options from local brands, and international stores. It is home to several heritage and other malls, including Robinsons, TANGS, ION Orchard, etc.

5b

Shopping

. . .

*Singapore,
a shopping
paradise*

___

SUNTEC CITY

It is a major mixed-use development with a shopping mall, office buildings, and a convention centre. Don't skip **Fountain of Wealth** listed by the Guinness Book of Records in 1998 as the largest fountain in the world.

APPLE MARINA BAY SANDS

It is a retail store selling Apple products and sits directly on the water. Company's most ambitious retail project was inspired by the Pantheon in Rome (an oculus in the center).

THE SHOPPES AT MARINA BAY SANDS

A collection of the latest fashion trends, with a majority of the shops offering luxury brands, newest technology, toys, etc.

5b

Shopping
Websites

6

Changi
Airport

Changi Airport
. . .
World's best airport
——

Changi Airport isn't just a travel hub, but also **a tourist destination** on its own, offering numerous attractions, like **Jewel**, a nature-themed entertainment and shopping complex.

Ranging from a variety of food offerings and shopping to visiting gardens and the greenery. You can also take special tours to experience Changi Airport.

Main attractions ▸

- **Forest Valley:** Featuring Rain Vortex with light & sound show by night
- **Slide@T3:** The slide that takes you to your gate

Map

- **Gardens & parks** like Butterfly & Sunflower Garden, Canopy Park
- **Coffee Museum:** learn the coffee heritage of Singapore
- **Five Spice:** Providing authentic street food
- **Movie theater:** global movies for free
- **Other:** free massages, snooze lounge, video games, playgrounds, a hotel, art like kinetic sculptures, etc.

i **Did you know?** Changi Airport has been named as the World's Best Airport for the eighth year in a row

Haw Par Villa
Website

Hell's
Museum

Haw Par Villa

· · ·

Asian cultural park

—

7

ENTRANCE FEE

Free

OPENING HOURS

9am-10pm

Daily

Location

Take everything you love about the Asian community, and you'll find it in this cultural park, one of the last of its kind. A rich heritage, history, and art is kept within this space with sheltered pavilions and events geared for the people. Haw Par Villais home to more than 1,000 statues and dioramas that show stories from **Chinese mythologies, folklore, and legends.**

The park also holds social events, performances, food and art markets, and even lifestyle activities such as yoga. Traditional Chinese architecture inspires many of its sculptures, decor, and pavilions. The park is a great way to discover the cultural heritage of Singapore.

Don't skip **Hell's Museum** to better understand Haw Par Villa's Ten Courts of Hell and much more.

i **Did you know?** The park was initially named after the Tiger Balm medical ointrnent that the owners' father invented. It was called the Tiger Balm Garden.

8

Singapore
Botanic
Gardens

Singapore Botanic Gardens
. . .
Over 160-year-old tropical garden
——

ENTRANCE FEE

Free

OPENING HOURS

5am - midnight
Daily

Location

The Singapore Botanic Gardens are a **UNESCO Heritage Site**. The gardens area popular placefor recreational activities such as jogging, or even bird watching.

Different attractions inside the 60-acre (24 ha) land include the **National Orchid Garden,** the SBG Heritage Museum, and the Jacob Ballas Children's Garden, free concerts in special outdoor auditorium, little tropical rainforest, **lakes** (Eco, Swan & Symphony), Saraca Stream, The Bandstand, rainforest trail, The Botany Centre, Keppel Discovery Wetlands, etc. There are also numerous choices for food & dining inside the garden.

You can enter the Botanic Garden from four entrances: Tanglin, Tyersall Gallop, Nassim, Bukit Timah.

i **Did you know?** The oldest tree in the garden is at least 150 years old and is called the Tembusu tree.

Food & Hawker Centers

. . .

Variety of food courts

9

The city-state sees food as essential to what Singapore is as a nation.

Although there are religious differences (Malay, Chinese, Indian, Indonesian and other cultures) and a large number of vegetarians or vegans, people respect one another. They still come together to eat.

Visit the **World's cheapest Michelin-starred meal** at Singapore's Liao Fan Hong Kong Soya Sauce Chicken Rice & Noodle. Here you'll try a delicious meal for a few dollars.

People prefer to eat at **hawker centers** or food courts as opposed to restaurants because of the variety they can get in food and hawker centers.

It is also much **more affordable** and can be found just about everywhere.

i **Don't miss:** One of the most famous hawker centers popular amongst tourists is Newton Food Centre, also featured in a Hollywood hit Crazy Rich Asians.

10a

Buy Tickets
Here

Gardens by the Bay

. . .

*A city
in a garden*

10a

OPENING HOURS
—

9am-9pm
Attractions
5am-2am
Outdoor Gardens

Garden Rhapsody
(light, sound show):
7^{45}pm & 8^{45}pm

Location

ENTRANCE FEE
—

Free (outside)
Attractions vary

Gardens by the Bay is a **haven for nature lovers,** offer 250 acres or 101 hectares and three different spaces to explore: Bay South, Bay East, and Bay Central Garden.

Gardens hope to spread the love for nature and green spaces.

There was an **international design competition** for the design of the garden in 2006. The organization received more than 70 entries from 24 countries.

i **Did you know?** Gardens by the Bay received multiple awards, like Best Attraction Experience.

10b

Gardens by the Bay

. . .

*A city
in a garden*

———

There are many amazing views to enjoy:

OCBC Skyway: A walkway that lets you see the part with a bird's eye view, hanging between two Supertrees and is 420 feet or 128 meters long.

Supertree Grove: If you want to see more of Marina Bay, you can walk this observatory on top of the tallest Supertree and see the sights from 164 feet or 50 meters up in the air.

DON'T MISS:

Kingfisher Wetlands: if you love nature and birds, this nature sanctuary is a place for you.

Garden Rhapsody: a lights and sounds show on the Supertrees.

Flower Dome: a collection of flowers from five continents (3 acres).

Cloud Forest: home to a breathtaking waterfall and some rare plants and vegetation. Don't skip **Avatar: The Experience**, an immersive walkthrough.

Floral Fantasy: a marriage of history, fantasy, and flowers, the design and floral art in this space are taken from numerous fairy tales and stories like the Hanging Gardens of Babylon.

10b

Buy Tickets
Here

Top 20
MAPS

10 Additional Things to Do in Singapore

This section includes:

11

Southern
Ridges

Henderson Waves

. . .

The highest pedestrian bridge in Singapore

———

11

ENTRANCE FEE

Free

OPENING HOURS

24/7

Location

A unique bridge that **looks like a wave** with its curves and twists, many features of the bridge can be explored. It is a part of **Southern Ridges** scenic walking path connecting to many parks with bridges, wildlife and stunning city views.

The bridge is supported by steel arches and has what may be described as ribs to make the shape of waves. Its **extraordinary design** results in hidden alcoves and nooks, where people can lounge and rest.

You can admire the structure by night. A lighting effect is placed on the bridge that makes it look even more stunning (between 7 pm and 7 am every night).

i **Tip:** Explore other parks in the area, like Mount Faber Park, Telok Blangah Hill Park and other parks.

12a

Museums

Museums
. . .
*Discover art
& culture*

12a

ArtScience Museum

A fusion of art & science, including topics on culture and technology, with 21 galleries. It showcases the best in art and science, featuring famous artists, innovations in science, **Future World** immersive exhibition and more.

National Museum of SG

The Singapore Living Galleries & History Gallery: The oldest museum in the city-state is distinct from its immersive experiences, diverse events, and classic architecture. Learn about the history and culture of Singapore.

Red Dot Design Museum

Based on the world-renowned Red Dot Design Award, it offers a wide range of exhibitions from the relationship of humans and nature, futuristic designs, and award winners of the prestigious award.

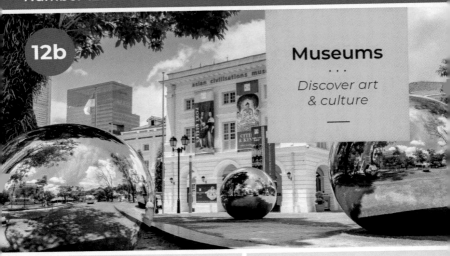

12b

Museums
. . .
*Discover art
& culture*
—

Asian Civilizations Museum: it is dedicated to the culture and history of Asian Civilizations. It spreads out on three stories, dedicated to trade, faith, belief, and materials and design.

National Gallery SG: it showcases over 8,000 Singaporean and Southeast Asian modern art and is the most extensive public collection.

Lee Kong Chian Natural History Museum: with a focus on Southeast Asian biodiversity, their collection has more than 2,000 natural history specimens and two museum gardens.

The Parkview Museum Singapore: it houses a collection of contemporary art that ranges from the largest selection of Salvador Dali's art outside of Spain, Chinese contemporary art, etc.

Indian Heritage Centre: with five permanent galleries that aim to combine traditional and modern Indian architecture. Its architecture and design were made to highlight the Indian culture.

Madame Tussauds Singapore: is a Wax museum with five different experiences located on Sentosa Island.

Vintage Cameras Museum: it is set in the form of a camera and a lens as an entry with around 1000 cameras.

12b

1940s

In early Singapore and Malaya, labour was not organised in the form of unions but guilds, which included employers and employees. It was only when the Trade Union Ordinance was passed in 1940 that trade unions were established.

Throughout Malaya and Singapore, workers did not organise themselves into labour unions until the 1940s. Before that, organised labour existed mainly in the form of Chinese guilds or *hongs*. These guilds started out as legitimate trade organisations comprising both workers and owners and existed in Singapore from as early as the 1820s. Later, the owners within each guild started recruiting *sighting men* to protect their interests but over time, many of these *sighting men* turned into criminal gangs or *secret societies* which were, to some extent, kept in check by the *Societies Ordinance 1868*.

by the *Straits Settlements* against unions were impractical. Their claims for workers of an impending war. This very idea sparked the very core and soon gave rise to an empowered and organised working...

It was only in 1959 that was introduced with Peeliked (Sidney Web from 1926 to 1931 in a Octos proposed that legislation be passed lawful for civil purposes and prototor the registration. In 1940, the Industrial Courts of the Trade Union Ordinance were...

rigins of
rade Unionism
Malaya and

Museums

Ride a Bumboat

· · ·

Discover Singapore from water

—

13

The boats have been preserved and are **now used as tourist boats** for cruises and tours.

Bumboat river tours are generally cheaper to get around and see the iconic Singapore landmarks.

The best time for a tour is during a late afternoon or at dusk to catch the sun setting on the river.

Discover downtown Singapore with its water taxi called Bumboat.

These are **small boats** that were initially **used in the 19th to 20th century** for trade and delivering supplies.

Singaporean bumboats are adapted from wooden European-style lighters and known locally as Twakows and Tongkangs.

i **Tip:** If you take a nighttime trip, you can admire the lights show at Marina Bay.

14

Merlion

...

A mythical creature & national symbol

___

14

Location

This mythical creature has the **head of a lion** and the **body of a fish** and represents Singapore and its people in various sports teams, tourism, and as a patriotic emblem.

The world Merlion combines the names "mer" (meaning sea) and "lion." Singapore was once a **fishing village**, and it was called Temasek, which translates as Sea Town in Javanese. An aquatic route, part of the larger Silk route that also passed through Temasek. The lion head represents **Singapura**, which is the Singapore's original name translated to **Lion City in Sanskrit**.

According to **Sang Nila Utama's legend**, a Malay prince was sailing across the sea and discovered a fishing island called Temasek. He met with a lion, a majestic creature that Singapura was named after (the Lion City). Sang Nila Utama was the founder of the Kingdom of Singapura in 1299.

The Merlion was **used as a logo** for tourism board and was designed by Fraser Brunner in 1964. He added a fishtail to the statue to suggest Singapore's humble beginnings as a fishing village.

i **Did you know?** There are six Merlion statues in Singapore and can also be found in other countries. **65**

15

Buy Tickets
Here

Singapore Flyer

. . .

Giant Observation Wheel

—

15

ENTRANCE FEE
—
S$33
25 USD | 23 EUR

OPENING HOURS
—
2pm-10pm
Daily

Location

This 42-story observation wheel provides a fantastic view of the city towards Marina Bay and Singapore River.

Singapore Flyer is **one of the largest observation wheels** in the world. It takes about 30 minutes for a full rotation.

At its top height, you can even see some far-located destinations like the Sentosa Island or parts of Malaysia or Indonesia.

Do some exploring in the **Retail Terminal** with shopping, dining, and other activities like a flight simulation or an art exhibition.

i **Did you know?** With 541 ft. (165 m) is bigger than the London Eye.

16

Jurong Lake Gardens

Jurong Lake Gardens

. . .

A garden surrounding a lake

———

16

ENTRANCE FEE

Free

OPENING HOURS

24/7

8^{30}am-6^{30}pm
Visitor Center

Location

Jurong Lake Gardens is a 222-acre or 90-hectare area that includes Lakeside Garden, Chinese and Japanese Gardens, and Garden Promenade. It is said to be a **people's garden**, a place where families can relax and enjoy a breath of fresh air.

There's a lot of nature to see here, with the center of the gardens being the **Jurong Lake**.

Don't miss these following attractions:

- **Rasau Walk:** A boardwalk where you can get close to the water and see many of the underwater plants
- **Grasslands:** You can see many bird species having tall grass as their natural habitat: they feed & seek shelter there
- **Alstonia Island & Freshwater Swamp Forest:** a variety of plants that grow in freshwater swamps.

i *Important!!!* Currently, the Chinese and Japanese Gardens are closed for redevelopment.

69

17

TreeTop
Walk

TreeTop Walk
· · ·
*Hanging bridge,
a part of
MacRitchie routes*
——

17

ENTRANCE FEE

Free

OPENING HOURS
——
8³⁰/9am-5pm
Tuesday-Sunday

Location

With a thousand birds and over 250 species, **suspension bridge** in MacRitchie Reservoir Park (Central Water Catchment) is a haven for bird lovers. The TreeTop Walk plays an important role in forest canopy research. The park has been modified to mimic the natural habitat of birds.

MacRitchie Reservoir Park is a popular place for nature lovers, runners, water sports enthusiasts & others.

There are **many activities** you can do here: rent a kayak from Paddle Lodge and explore the reservoir, go freshwater fishing, go hiking on one of many trails, climb the Jelutong Tower observation deck, and more.

i **Important!!!** Walking the MacRitchie Trail, including the TreeTop Walk and back, takes about 3 to 5 hours. **71**

18

Buy Tickets
Here

Staycation in
the Wild

Singapore Zoo

. . .

World's best rainforest zoo

——

18

ENTRANCE FEE
——
S$48
36 USD | 34 EUR

OPENING HOURS
——
8³⁰am-6pm
Daily

Location

Explore some of the nature and wildlife that Singapore has to offerand visit the Singapore Zoo. It features 11 different zones with **over 300 species**. Some of the zones are the Australasia Exhibit, the Primate Kingdom, and Reptile Garden, among others.

The zoo is designed for the animals to have space and an environment that **mimics their natural habitat**. There are also activities for the little ones with the Rainforest Kidzworld. You can get up-close with some of the animals and enjoy a water park inside.

The 64-acre or 26-hectare park sees about 1.9 million visitors per year.

i **Don't miss:** The Night Safari - world's first nocturnal zoo or even stay in an outdoor dome tent (Staycation in the Wild). **73**

19

Visit their
website

Esplanade Theatres on the Bay

. . .

Arts venue with concert hall, theatre & mall

___

19

Location

Esplanade – Theatres on the Bay is a **cultural hub** in Singapore and a popular destination for locals and tourists. It was opened in 2002 as a performing arts center consisting of a concert hall, theater, theater studio, and outdoor performance spaces. The center hosts various performances, including music, dance, theater, and more.

The concert hall features outstanding acoustics and is home to the **Singapore Symphony Orchestra**. The theater is a flexible space that can be used for various performances, including plays and musicals. The theater studio is a smaller space used for experimental and intimate performances. The center also features an outdoor stage for free community performances.

The building's design was inspired by traditional Malay architecture, and it features a distinctive roof that resembles the rippling skin of a durian (spiky and stinky tropical fruit), hence the **nickname "The Durian."**

i **Tip:** embark on Esplanade Tour that takes you into the Concert Hall, Theatre, and more.

Wetlands

. . .

Mangroves and swamps rich in biodiversity

____

20

Location

Although a small island, Singapore has many natural spots, hidden walking trails and other interesting areas to offer. One of them is **wetlands**, home to a variety of flora and fauna.

Visit at least one of the most interesting ones, where you can even observe birds, explore mangroves with a kayak, or embark on other interesting activities.

- **Sungei Buloh Wetland Reserve:** Singapore's first ASEAN Heritage Park. It offers extensive mangrove forest, mudflats, ponds, hiking trails, and mid-canopy walk & pods, art classes, etc.
- **Learning Forest** in SG Botanic Gardens offers freshwater forest wetland to a lowland rainforest with many elevated walkways and other boardwalks.
- **Khatib Bongsu Nature Park**, popular for mangroves kayaking
- **Chek Jawa Wetlands** (Pulau Ubin) spanning across 100 hectares and features, boardwalk, observation tower & a Visitor Centre.

i **Tip:** Explore also constructed wetlands, like Sengkang Riverside Park or beautiful Punggol Waterways

Itineraries & Things to Do

This section includes:

ITINERARIES

To make your trip to Singapore stress-free and organized, we prepared a simple one, two, and three-day itineraries.

Each suggested itinerary includes a dedicated link to customized Google Map that you can easily use on your phone.

◄ MAP

1-Day Itinerary

Morning

- Visit unique districts, like Kampong Glam with Sultan Mosque, Haji Lane and other places
- Explore Little India with Buffalo Road, Indian Heritage Centre and House of Tan Teng Niah
- If time: explore Chinatown with Complex Food Centre, Pagoda Street, etc.

Afternoon

- Raffles Landing - if time
- Explore Marina Bay: Merlion Park, Waterfront Promenade, SkyPark Observation Deck (if time), Helix Bridge
- Visit Gardens by the Bay: Cloud Forest,...

Evening

Garden Rhapsody

2-Day Itinerary

MAP ▶

Day 1

Morning

- Explore Chinatown with Complex Food Centre, Pagoda Street, etc.
- If time: Fullerton Hotel, Cavenagh Bridge, Raffles Landing Site, Asian Civilisations Mus.

Afternoon

- Explore Marina Bay: Merlion Park, Waterfront Promenade, SkyPark Observation Deck (if time), Helix Bridge & other attractions
- Visit Gardens by the Bay: Cloud Forest, many gardens, OCBC Skyway

Evening

Camden Town

Day 2

Morning

- Walk around Fort Canning Park and explore its many gardens, The Battlebox, Fort Gate, National Museum of Singapore, etc.
- If time: Clarke Quay & Old Police Station

Afternoon & Evening

- Explore Bugis Street with famous market, Bugis+ and Bugis Junktion
- Visit Kampong Glam with Sultan Mosque, Haji Lane and other places
- If time: Little India with Buffalo Road, Indian Heritage Centre and House of Tan Teng Niah
- Explore Orchard Road shopping areas and its bars and clubs

◄ MAP

3-Day Itinerary

Day 1

Morning

- Visit Chinatown with hawker centers, Pagoda St., etc.
- If time: Raffles Landing Site

Afternoon & Evening

- Explore Marina Bay: Merlion Park, Waterfront Promenade, SkyPark Obs.Deck, Helix Bridge, etc.
- Gardens by the Bay: e.g., Cloud Forest, Garden Rhapsody

Day 2

Morning

- Fort Canning Park: The Battlebox, Fort Gate, gardens, etc.
- If time: Clarke Quay & Old Police Station

Day 2 - continue

Afternoon & Evening

- Explore Bugis Street
- Visit Kampong Glam & Haji Lane
- If time: Little India
- Explore Orchard Rd. shopping areas and its bars and clubs

Day 3

Morning

- SG Botanic Gardens with its many lakes, gardens, etc.
- Haw Par Villa

Afternoon & Evening

- If time: Henderson Waves & surrounding parks
- Spend an afternoon at Sentosa Island and enjoy Magical Shores or Wing of Time in the evening

Activities
& Links

Things to do...

...IF IT'S TOO HOT

- Spend a day at the beach: Siloso Beach at Sentosa Island
- Waterparks like Adventure Cove Waterpark
- Visit parks & gardens: Botanic Gardens, Gardens by the Bay
- Go hiking at Southern Ridges (Henderson Waves) or take MacRitchie Trail (TreeTop Walk)
- Do some sports, like paddleboard, zipline, bungy jump, jet ski, etc.
- Take a river cruise or a boat ride
- Rooftop bars & eateries, like Loof, Lantern or LeVeL33

...IF IT'S RAINING

- Gardens by the Bay: Cloud Forest, etc.
- Go shopping at ION Orchard, Bugis+, The Shoppes at Marina Bay Sands
- Try indoor skydiving iFly Singapore
- Indoor skating at HiRoller
- Attend art class at Artify Studio
- PasarBella farmers market
- Visit museums
- Visit S.E.A. Aquarium
- Visit unique bars, like Kreams Krafthouse, Central Perk, etc.
- Visit Heaven Spot – graffiti art studio

Things to do...

...IN THE EVENING

- Attend one of many shows at Esplanade, Singapore Repertory Theatre, Ngee Ann Kongsi Theatre, etc.
- Enjoy Garden Rhapsody, a lights and sounds show on the Supertrees at Gardens by the Bay
- Go to a bar or a restaurant: The Old Man, Tippling Club, Lantern, 1-Altitude, Potato Head Singapore, etc.
- Embark on an evening or a night tour: Chinatown Trishaw Night Tour, on a night safari, Night Out @ Marina Bay

...WITH KIDS

- Visit Singapore Discovery Centre
- Enjoy indoor play-grounds, like Khatib Clubhouse
- Water parks like HydroDash, Wild Wild Wet, etc.
- Universal Studios
- Canopy Park
- Singapore Zoo
- Enjoy Snow City, Singapore's first indoor snow centre with many activities
- Science Centre Singapore
- Jacob Ballas Children's Garden
- Admiralty Park
- SEA Aquarium
- Forest Adventure recreation center

Singapore Travel Guide by Hungry Passport
4225 Solano Ave. Ste 63, Napa CA 94558, USA

www.hungrypassport.xyz

Disclaimer: While we do our best to provide the most current information, opening hours change on a regular basis, businesses close, etc. so we do not guarantee any information in this travel guide is accurate. If you are in doubt, always research on your own. We are not endorsed by any business or other entity presented in this guide.

CREDITS: Cover photo: Adobe Stock | P2: Hungry Passport Travel Guide page mockups, Envato (scanning QR code, mobile phone), Google Maps | P4: Adobe Stock and Hungry Passport | P6: Envato | P7: 123rf (power plugs & outlet style graphics) | P8 (from above): Adobe Stock, Envato, Envato | P9: Envato (Weather Icons) | P10: Adobe Stock | P18: Twenty20 | P19: Envato (top), Twenty20 (bottom) | P20: Twenty20 P10: Adobe Stock | P13: Adobe Stock | P15: Twenty20 | P16: Envato (top), Twenty20 (bottom) | P18: Twenty20 | P24: Hungry Passport | P25: Hungry Passport | P26: Adrian Jakob/Unsplash | P27: Hungry Passport | P28 (from above): Twenty20, Twenty20, Twenty20 | P29: Chapman Chow/Unsplash | P30: Hungry Passport | P31: Envato (top), Twenty20 (bottom) | P32: Hungry Passport (top), Adobe Stock (bottom) | P33: Hungry Passport | P34: Adobe Stock | P35: Adobe Stock | P36 (from above): Adobe Stock, Hungry Passport, Hungry Passport, Hungry Passport | P37: Hungry Passport | P38: Twenty20 | P39 (from above): Hungry Passport, Twenty20, Hungry Passport, Twenty20 | P40 (from above): Twenty20, Ahmad Affandi Lubis/ Pixabay, Twenty20, Twenty20 | P41: Twenty20 | P42: Adobe Stock | P43: Adobe Stock | P44: Vinson Tan/ Pixabay | P45: Adobe Stock | P46: Twenty20 | P47: Adobe Stock | P48: Twenty20 | P49: Adobe Stock (top), Envato (bottom) | P50: Adobe Stock | P51: Envato (top), Envato (bottom) | P52: Twenty20 (top), Envato (bottom) | P53: Twenty20 | P56: Adobe Stock | P57: Adobe Stock | P58: Twenty20 | P59 (from above): Twenty20, Envato, Hungry Passport, Hungry Passport | P60: Adobe Stock | P61: Joyce Romero/Unsplash | P62: Adobe Stock | P63: Envato (top), Bernd Hildebrandt/ Pixabay (bottom) | P64: Adobe Stock | P65: Envato | P66: Adobe Stock | P67: Adobe Stock | P68: David Kubovsky/Unsplash | P69: Adobe Stock | P70: Adobe Stock | P71: Twenty20 | P72: Ludwig Kwan/Pexels | P73: Twenty20 | P74: Adobe Stock | P75: Adobe Stock | P76: Adobe Stock | P77: Adobe Stock | P83: Adobe Stock | P84: Twenty20 | P87: Adobe Stock | Back cover: Hungry Passport Travel Guide mockup, Envato (scanning QR code) | Icons throughout this guide: Envato & Hungry Passport